DRAWINGS

EDITED BY JOHN REWALD

A BITTNER ART BOOK

NEW YORK · THOMAS YOSELOFF · LONDON

TO THE MEMORY OF PAUL DURAND-RUEL

INE AND COLOR APPEARED, DURING THE
first half of the nineteenth century, to be two irreconcilable enemies. The violent dis-
cussions about the exclusive advantages of the one or the other, which raged among the
followers of Ingres and of Delacroix, only widened the gap without offering a solution.
While Ingres, in his stubborn emphasis on linear perfection, came close to considering
a painting merely as a colored drawing, Delacroix's febrile brush superbly disregarded
the precision of conventional contours. But his manner of drawing with his brush so that
stroke and color would be one, his ability to use line as an expression of movement rather
than as the limitation of sharply defined objects, failed to convince his contemporaries
that a colorist did not need to be ignorant of drawing.

It was Baudelaire's merit to affirm — what might then have appeared heresy — that
"there are two types of drawing: the drawing of the colorists and the drawing of the
draftsmen. The procedures are inverted, but one may draw well with frenzied color just
as one may obtain harmonious masses of color while remaining exclusively a draftsman."
Baudelaire, however, did not go so far as to denounce completely the arbitrary division
of line and color. When Ingres' linear accomplishments inspired him to assert that "the
draftsman is a colorist who has missed his calling," he seems to have been unintentionally
questioning the true nature of Delacroix's genius, that of being equally an accomplished
draftsman and an accomplished colorist.

Whereas Ingres considered draftsmanship an end in itself, Delacroix's superiority lay
in the fact that he was a painter in the full sense of the word. Unwilling to commit himself to any narrow program, refusing to accept any classifications, he conceived drawing
and color to be inseparable in painting. Delacroix's creative impulse produced a whole,
and in this whole there was no drawing independent of composition and color; no com-

[7]

position without color and drawing; no color which did not condition drawing and composition. It was the perfect fusion of these elements, at a time when official teaching was careful to divide them, which attracted the younger generation seeking to escape sterile academism. Delacroix's complete liberty of expression, his brilliant command of his medium and the easy flow of his inspiration, unhampered by any cold purposefulness, offered a stimulating example to those who feared that Ingres' rigid principles led to nothing more than skill. Ingres' linear mastery, attained through the complete sacrifice of imagination, confined within the limits of tradition and prejudice, was rich in virtues but poor in life. Delacroix caught, even in his lightest sketches, the vital spark. "He is not only a great draftsman of form," Gauguin once wrote, "but also an innovator; line is for him a medium to accentuate an idea."

Among those who turned to Delacroix in the decisive years of their apprenticeship was Auguste Renoir. Like Manet and Cézanne — and later Gauguin and van Gogh — he copied the master's work. However, his admiration for Delacroix by no means blinded him to Ingres' merits. In fact, Renoir was the only painter of the second half of the nineteenth century who frankly acknowledged his debt to both Delacroix and Ingres. Whereas the former guided his early steps and assisted him in establishing a link with the past, with Rubens and Watteau, the latter helped to extricate him from complex difficulties when he felt, many years later, the need for structure and line. But at the time when he turned to Ingres, Renoir already possessed the one quality the development of which he owed to Delacroix, spontaneity, and this rescued him from dangerous submission to linear proficiency. Ingres delivered him only after Delacroix had saved him. Thus Renoir combined two heritages and reconciled the two poles, color and line.

Renoir's beginnings differed very little from those of the many who followed conventional art courses, except that he showed great facility and also some inclination to use color more freely than his teachers liked. None of his early drawings have been preserved; he may have destroyed them, just as he destroyed certain canvases as soon as he had liberated himself from the academic yoke. He had no sooner left the Ecole des Beaux-Arts than he turned toward Courbet, whose forceful execution and strong contrasts, whose heavy volumes and simplified drawing, offered entirely new aspects. It was only after having worked for some time as a follower of Courbet, after having tested various modes of expression, that he discovered the subtle qualities of Delacroix. By then he had experience enough to realize that these qualities truly corresponded to his own sensibility. Delacroix thus became his master by preference, chosen not by chance but from the conviction of deep affinities.

[8]

What attracted Renoir in Delacroix's art was above all his color, his technique and—inseparable from them—the fierce vibrations of his drawing. Nothing could have better prepared him for the new approach to nature upon which he engaged, together with his friend Monet, and which was to lead eventually to impressionism. The farther he advanced toward an instantaneous retention of sensations, the more he abandoned whatever influence the principles of the Ecole des Beaux-Arts might have had upon him, the less he was preoccupied with linear expression.

For the first time in the history of art, perhaps, Monet and his group insisted on a pursuit of impressions in so direct a way that preliminary sketches became unnecessary, in fact, would have appeared a negation of their efforts. More than Delacroix had ever done, the impressionists considered drawing dependent upon color and represented their perceptions in a dense tissue of color touches never divided by incisive strokes. There was no need for linear demarcation, since form could be suggested in its fullness through color modulation alone. Nature observed on the spot offered a minimum of lines, and even these appeared unstable, broken by reverberations of their surroundings, pulverized by ever changing plays of light.

Baudelaire had already stated that nature did not offer immutable contours. "A good drawing," he had written, "is not a hard, cruel, despotic, motionless line enclosing a form like a straitjacket. Drawing should be like nature, living and restless. Simplification in drawing is a monstrosity; nature shows us an endless series of curved, fleeting, broken lines, according to an unerring law of generation, in which parallels are always undefined and meandering, and concaves and convexes correspond to and pursue each other."

The impressionists went further: they denied that lines existed in nature. They refused to see a contour where an object presented its profile; they were preoccupied with the appearance of its form under specific conditions. They declined to isolate it from its surroundings; they professed no interest in it, except as part of a whole, as a receptacle of iridescence. They perceived colored masses and studied their interactions; they ignored the limits of forms and planes, since light ignores them and weaves them together.

No wonder, then, that Monet and Sisley, for instance, hardly ever made drawings. Renoir, the impressionist, seems also to have drawn very little. He seldom used his pencil but occasionally worked with pastel crayons which permitted him to obtain results similar to his paintings. From time to time he drew in pen and ink, endeavoring to achieve a texture of vibrant hatchings. What preoccupied him was not the arabesque of a contour but the creation of mellow forms through the delicate interplay of light and shadows.

It seems possible that a fortuitous circumstance—the founding of the weekly, *La Vie*

Moderne, by Renoir's patrons, the Charpentiers—prompted the painter to do more drawings than before and to do them from an entirely new angle. The first issue of this publication, devoted to artistic, literary and mundane life, with a marked tendency toward the popular, appeared in April 1879. Renoir's brother Edmond, a professional journalist, was on the staff, and the painter himself ranked among the illustrators. Anxious to be of service to his benefactress, Mme Charpentier, Renoir accepted all kinds of commissions. He drew portraits of prominent people for the cover, made drawings after some paintings (among them Manet's *Fifre*), designed initials and even declared himself ready to make sketches for a special fashion page by visiting various milliners and dressmakers and by drawing hats and gowns in their shops. This proposal was not accepted, possibly because there was no space, and Renoir was entrusted instead with such chores as meeting the famous ballerina Rosita Mauri, who graciously "lent" her head for portraiture but left to a less famous colleague the task of assuming a tiring ballet pose.

Renoir enjoyed greater freedom in his work whenever he undertook to illustrate for *La Vie Moderne* some short stories by his brother. Here he could abandon himself to his imagination and even use some of his paintings for inspiration, as he did in two drawings of dancing couples, obviously done after recently completed canvases of the same subject. Moreover, these drawings were reproduced more faithfully, according to a new process, while his first illustrations for *La Vie Moderne* had had to be done on a special, grained paper, on which white was obtained by scraping, an awkward technique called "guillotage."

While he worked occasionally for *La Vie Moderne* between 1879 and 1886, Renoir's real interest lay in his painting, where he suddenly felt himself confronted with new problems. He had arrived at a phase where luminous spots and capricious effects of reflection began to menace the unity of his composition, where the observation of instantaneous changes threatened to destroy his contact with the objects themselves. Fearing that impressionism might lead him toward a complete dissolution of volumes, he sensed a danger which he tried to escape. Whereas Monet was prepared to go the whole way, to follow his sensations even to the point where the subject itself was ignored beyond its light-bathed surface, Renoir felt the need for more emphasis on structure. Unwilling to stray altogether from the path of tradition, he endeavored to re-establish relationship with the "simplicity and grandeur of the ancient painters."

The works of Raphael drew Renoir to Italy. In 1881-82 he went to Rome and Naples, to study there the frescoes by Ingres' idol, as well as Pompeian painting. They made a profound impression upon him. In front of Raphael's compositions he sighed: "Unlike me, he did not seek the impossible," and he observed with some surprise that the master had been able to study the effects of light without ever having worked out-of-doors. Renoir began to wonder whether he had followed the right path and particularly regretted having too much neglected drawing.

TWO BATHERS · CA 1890

ATER RENOIR ACKNOWLEDGED THAT
"around 1883 [he was then in his early forties] a sort of break occurred in my work. I
had gone to the end of impressionism and I was reaching the conclusion that I didn't
know how either to paint or to draw. In a word, I was at a dead end." He destroyed some
paintings and was seized by an actual hatred for impressionism. As an antidote, he
painted several canvases in which every detail—including the leaves of trees—was first
carefully drawn with pen and ink on the canvas before he took up his brush. A number
of watercolors were done in the same fashion, that is, color was *added* to more or less
complete drawings; it was not part of them but played the rôle of a supplementary decoration. For three years Renoir labored at a large composition of bathers for which he did
a great number of preparatory drawings, the kind of drawing he had never done before.
It was the linear aspect of this composition which preoccupied him most, a contour both
sinuous and stylized, naive and ingenious at the same time. His color became cold and
almost crude, confined within the boundaries of precise outlines, no longer vibrating in
unison with light-bathed volumes.

Turning toward line as a means of discipline, Renoir applied himself to simplifying
forms at the expense of color. Like Ingres—whom he understood better after having
admired Raphael—he tried to imprison breathing forms in rigorous contours, sometimes
simple, sometimes even elegant, but occasionally also reminiscent of that linear "straitjacket" of which Baudelaire had spoken. So complete was the change in his work that
many friends viewed Renoir's evolution with alarm, while others hailed in him the true
inheritor of a great tradition. The rumors which spread about his new style are reflected
in an article by George Moore, who asserted that for two years Renoir had "laboured in
the life class, working on an average from seven to ten hours a day, and in two years he
had utterly destroyed every trace of the charming and delightful art which had taken

him twenty years to build up." And Moore added, somewhat patronizingly: "I know of no more tragic story."

There was, however, nothing tragic in Renoir's development. With admirable lucidity and will-power he fought against his spontaneity, and what he lost in charm he gained in grandeur. When he eventually became aware of the fact that he would never completely defeat his spontaneity — the most precious of his gifts — he decided to abandon his onesided emphasis on line. "Honor to you, Renoir, for not having feared to commit an error!" Rouault later exclaimed. Indeed, Renoir might have erred in allowing himself to be inspired by Raphael and Ingres; but an error admitted is no longer an error — it may even become a virtue.

When Renoir abandoned what has been called his "Ingresque" period, he was not only richer in experience, he was ready to be himself. Far from returning to where he had left off when he first went to Italy, he found himself on a new threshold, ready to combine his colorist's instinct with his draftsman's knowledge. Of impressionism he retained merely the glistening textures, the technique of small strokes, with which he now endeavored to create voluminous forms. He modeled with color, and though he did not rely on line, neither did he ignore it. Like Delacroix he achieved the perfect unity of color and line. But while the former's concern had been with movement, Renoir's was with plasticity.

Having found a way to unite color and line, Renoir discovered the whole range of possibilities offered by each. He began to consider drawings as works in themselves. They were no longer reproductions of his own paintings or occasional sketches to which he himself attached little importance, nor were they preparatory studies for his compositions. Line became a new medium for him, but, reluctant to separate it completely from color, he used chalks, of which sanguine became his favorite, from time to time livened by white highlights or by black accents. His sanguines were drawn, as has been said, "in flesh and blood."

Though sanguines occupy an important place among Renoir's late drawings — he actually revived this almost forgotten medium dear to Watteau, Boucher, Fragonard — the artist did not have to rely upon red chalks for color effects. Even in his black and white drawings, executed with charcoal or with greasy pencils, he knew how to obtain a wide range of modulations and particularly a velvety quality of intense black. With these he achieved pictorial effects which put his late drawings in a category by themselves. Not only his red, but also his black is rich, powerful and subtle; both are used for color as well as for line.

[13]

With his soft chalks Renoir crushed lines, blurred contours and modeled forms. Occasionally he wiped a number of strokes into large areas. Often several lines, repeating themselves in parallel, generate a vibrating form. Thus the human bodies, which he conceived as sensuous and generous, overflow their outlines and radiate into space. Line is no longer a limit which separates an object from its surroundings, it is, on the contrary, the medium that unites them. If it sets off a voluminous form against its background, it also creates between background and form that suggestion of space which gives the body its expansive roundness, its plenitude.

It was no accident that the aging Renoir went even further in his longing for plasticity, that he turned to sculpture, though his crippled hands were almost incapable of modeling. Just as sculpture projects itself into space, absorbs it, participates in it, so his drawings approach the model not as a pretext for arabesques but as an object that turns around, that quivers with life and movement. And he obtained this quivering, less by careful imitation of the plays of light and shadow, than through the spontaneity with which he threw onto paper those colorful lines full of suggestive power, of subtle values, of warm feeling and of radiant joy.

Baudelaire would not have failed to recognize that Renoir's sanguines and black and white sketches answered his definition that a drawing ought to be like nature, living and restless, rich with curved, fleeting, broken lines, with parallels undefined and meandering, with concaves and convexes that correspond to and pursue each other. Yet, though Renoir's late drawings conform to Baudelaire's conception, they are not primarily linear expressions. Renoir the draftsman was not, like Ingres, a "colorist who has missed his calling." He created a new kind of drawing in which a passionate harmony of mass, volume and color emerges from strokes of chalk.

LIST OF PLATES

The plates have been arranged chronologically, as far as possible. Where there is no indication of size or of owner, this information has not been available to the author.

ing: "Toutes les six, se tenant par les bras, occupant la largeur des chaussées, s'en allaient, vêtues de clair, avec des rubans noués autour de leurs cheveux nus. L'Assommoir, page 453. Emile Zola."

Renoir's drawing, though it catches admirably the atmosphere of a Parisian boulevard, may have appeared too charming and light for Zola's robust text, and this may account for the fact that the project was never realized. It is possible, however, that the drawing was intended merely as an illustration for an excerpt of *L'Assommoir*, to be published in *La Vie Moderne*, but, contrary to an indication in the catalogue of the exhibition of "Masterdrawings," Albright Art Gallery, Buffalo, N. Y., 1935, it never appeared in this periodical.

5

HEAD OF A YOUNG GIRL, 1875
PASTEL, 19¾ x 15½"
Glasgow Art Gallery (Burrell Collection).
This pastel as well as the three following may have been included in Renoir's first one-man show, held in 1879 in the gallery of *La Vie Moderne*, where the artist exhibited mostly pastels.

6

HEAD OF A YOUNG GIRL, 1875-79
PASTEL, 13⅜ x 10¼"
Collection R. A. Peto, England.

7

HEAD OF A YOUNG GIRL, 1875-79
PASTEL, 23⅝ x 16½"

8

HEAD OF A YOUNG GIRL, 1875-79
PASTEL, 11¾ x 9½"

9

THE DANCER ROSITA MAURI, 1881-83
CRAYON, 10¼ x 8¼
Kleemann Gallery, New York.

This drawing was published in *La Vie Moderne*, December 22, 1883.

10

ROSITA MAURI IN "LA FARANDOLE," 1881-83
Collection Paul Rosenberg.

According to the recollections of Jeanniot (see G. Jeanniot: "Souvenirs sur Degas," *Revue Universelle*, Oct.-Nov. 1933), the dancer posed in 1881 in the studio of Degas' friend, Viscount Lepic. She was accompanied by a young pupil of the Corps de Ballet who posed in various attitudes while the ballerina offered only her head for portraiture. Jeanniot went to sketch her for *La Vie Moderne* in the company of a colleague whom he does not name but who can have been none other than Renoir. Indeed, the present drawing shows some lack of adjustment between head and body. It was published in *La Vie Moderne*, December 22, 1883. (The size of the reproduction was 10¼ x 8".)

11

PORTRAIT OF RICHARD WAGNER, 1882-83

This drawing was made after a portrait of the musician which Renoir painted in January 1882 in Sicily (now in the Bibliothèque de l'Opéra, Paris). It was reproduced in *La Vie Moderne*, February 24, 1883, and had probably been done especially to illustrate an obituary of Wagner. (The size of the reproduction was 7 x 5½".)

Concerning his portrait painting, Renoir wrote from Palermo to a friend: "Wagner was very jolly and I very nervous and sorry I was not Ingres. I believe I used the time well; thirty-five minutes is not much. But if I had stopped before it would have been very beautiful, for toward the end my model lost his good humor and became stiff. I followed too closely this change. . . . Afterward Wagner wanted to see. He said: 'Ah! Ah! I look like a Protestant priest,' which was true. . . ."

Wagner is also supposed to have said—but not to Renoir—that the portrait was like "an embryo of an angel which an epicurean had swallowed, thinking it was an oyster." (See E. Lockspeiser: "The Renoir Portraits of Wagner," *Music and Letters*, January 1937.)

Another Renoir sketch of Wagner, in oils, is in the

collection of Alfred Cortot. Renoir also drew a portrait of the composer after a photograph from c. 1865 (but his drawing must have been done some twenty years later), which is reproduced in A. Jullien: *Richard Wagner, sa vie et ses oeuvres,* Paris, 1886, p. 157 and was probably made for this book. Jullien was a friend of Fantin-Latour with whom Renoir shared in his youth an ardent admiration for Wagner.

12

PORTRAIT OF PAUL CEZANNE, 1880
PASTEL, 20¾ x 16¾"

Durand-Ruel Galleries, New York.

This portrait, among the most important ones of Cézanne, was apparently done in Paris. Cézanne liked it well enough to copy it (see L. Venturi: *Cézanne, son art, son oeuvre,* Paris, 1936, No. 372), but did not succeed in reproducing its human warmth and directness. Renoir later used this portrait for a medallion of his friend, issued in bronze by Vollard, which today adorns a small fountain in Cézanne's native town, Aix-en-Provence. In 1902 Renoir also did a lithograph after this portrait (see L. Delteil: *Le peintre graveur illustré,* tome XVII, Paris, 1923, Renoir, No. 34).

13

LA DANSE A LA CAMPAGNE, 1883
CRAYON

Sketch for Renoir's painting of the same title, dated 1883 (in the Durand-Ruel collection). This painting rates among the first works denoting the artist's abandonment of impressionism and his emphasis on linear composition. The dancers are Edmond Renoir and Suzanne Valadon.

14

YOUNG WOMAN STANDING, c. 1880
CRAYON, 17¼ x 9¾"

Collection César de Hauke.

It has been supposed that this sketch represents the actress Jeanne Samary, of whom Renoir painted several portraits around 1880, but it may also show Suzanne Valadon, who posed for *La Danse à la Campagne,* or one of the artist's favorite models of that same time, Angèle. Whoever she was, to her apply the words which a contemporary critic wrote about one of Renoir's portraits of Jeanne Samary: "I felt as if the painter had seen her not in this world, nor yet in any dreary region of the dead, but in some cheerful elysium of light and color adapted to her merry and kindly genius." (P. G. Hamerton, 1891.)

15

LA DANSE A LA CAMPAGNE, 1883
CRAYON, 9½ x 4¾"
Collection César de Hauke.

This sketch for or after the painting of the same title was given by Renoir to his friend Portier, with a dedication which was effaced by the latter when the drawing was sold.

16

LA DANSE A LA CAMPAGNE, 1883
CRAYON, 19¼ x 13¼"
Honolulu Academy of Arts, Hawaii.

17

LA DANSE A LA CAMPAGNE, 1883
PEN AND INK, 15 x 7¼"

Collection Henry P. McIlhenny, Philadelphia, Pa.

This drawing was done after another version of Renoir's painting of the same title (now in the Museum of Fine Arts, Boston), to be used as an illustration for a short story by Paul Lhote, *Mademoiselle Zélia.* It bears in Renoir's handwriting a quotation from the passage to which it alludes: "elle valsait délicieusement abandonnée entre les bras d'un blond aux allures de canotier." It was published in *La Vie Moderne,* November 3, 1883 and is here reproduced after this publication.

There exist two *vernis-mou* etchings of the same subject, done supposedly around 1890 (see L. Delteil, *op. cit.,* Nos. 1, 2).

18

LA DANSE A LA CAMPAGNE, 1883
Collection Paul Rosenberg.

This drawing was apparently done *after* Renoir's

painting of the same title. It was published in *La Vie Moderne*, January 26, 1884. (The size of the illustration was 12¼ x 7").

19

COUPLE IN THE STREET, 1883
PEN AND BLACK CHALK, 17⅝ x 11½"

Fogg Museum of Art, Cambridge, Mass. (Winthrop Bequest).

Published in *La Vie Moderne* as illustration for Paul Lhote's short story, *Un idéal,* December 8, 1883. According to Renoir's brother, the artist always complained about the difficulty of drawing a man wearing a hat.

20

COUPLE ON A HILLSIDE, 1883
CRAYON, 16½ x 11⅛"

Collection Mrs. J. H. Rosenbaum, New York.

Edmond Renoir posed for this drawing on a rocky lane leading from Menton (where the two brothers stayed in 1883) to Castellar. It was done as illustration for a short story of Edmond's, *L'Etiquette,* which appeared in *La Vie Moderne,* December 29, 1883.

21

ANGLERS ALONG THE SEINE, 1883

This humorous drawing—unique of its kind among the works of Renoir—was done as title-page for some writings of his brother, an enthusiastic angler and an authority on the subject. It offers a panoramic view of the Seine in and around Paris, with a number of familiar monuments and bridges, like Notre-Dame and the Trocadéro, the Pont du jour and the Machine de Marly, etc. The reproduction was made after a galley proof in the possession of the late Edmond Renoir, according to whose recollections it appeared in 1883 in *Le Figaro* with an article on "La pêche à travers Paris." This page is said to have obtained a great success.

22

THE BEACH OF GUERNSEY, 1883
CRAYON, C. 12 X 20"

Private collection, France.

This drawing, as well as the following, seems to be related to Renoir's painting, *By the Seashore,* dated 1883, now in the Metropolitan Museum of Art, New York. Both drawings formerly belonged to Edmond Renoir.

23

THE BEACH OF GUERNSEY, 1883
CRAYON, C. 12 X 20"

Private collection, France.

From Guernsey Renoir wrote in September 1883 to his dealer Durand-Ruel: "Nothing is nicer than all these men and women closely mingled on the rocks. One has much more the impression of being in a landscape by Watteau than of reality." The freedom with which the artist has sketched the children in the background, however, seems more reminiscent of Daumier than of Watteau.

24

EDMOND RENOIR IN MENTON, 1883
Collection Paul Rosenberg.

This drawing was done as illustration for a short story by Edmond Renoir, *L'Etiquette,* and appeared in *La Vie Moderne,* December 15, 1883.

25

ORANGE VENDER, 1885-90
SANGUINE, 15¾ X 11"

26

WOMAN IN A ROCKING CHAIR, 1881-83
CHARCOAL AND PENCIL, 14¼ X 12"

Art Institute, Chicago (Samuel P. Avery Fund).

The watermark of the paper reads: "J. Whatman/ Turkey Mill/ 1881."

27

COPY AFTER MANET'S "FIFRE," 1883
CRAYON, 14½ x 9"

Wildenstein and Co., Inc., New York.

This drawing, which appeared in *La Vie Moderne,* January 12, 1884, was made upon the occasion of a memorial exhibition of Manet's work, held less than a year after the painter's death, at the Ecole des Beaux-Arts in Paris.

28

BATHER, 1881
PENCIL, 10⅝ x 6½"

This drawing was done for or after the painting of a *Bather,* dated 1881 and supposedly executed in Naples, which is now in the collection of Sir Kenneth Clark, London.

29

BATHER, c. 1885
SANGUINE, 16¾ x 12¼"

Art Institute, Chicago (Gift of Robert Allerton).

30

VENUS (LE PHENOMENE FUTUR), 1887
PEN AND INK, 6¾ x 4½"

An etching of the same subject was used as frontispiece for Mallarmé's *Pages,* Brussels, 1891, and possibly done especially for this purpose (see L. Delteil, *op. cit.* No. 3). It seems to illustrate the poet's lines: "A la place du vêtement vain, elle a un corps; et les yeux, semblables aux pierres rares! ne valent pas ce regard qui sort de sa chair heureuse: des seins levés comme s'ils étaient pleins d'un lait éternel, la pointe vers le ciel, aux jambes lisses qui gardent le sel de la mer première."

31

BATHER, 1883
PENCIL, 11⅝ x 7¾"

32

STUDY FOR "THE BATHERS," 1883
PENCIL, 8⅞ x 14"

Formerly Collection Marcel Guérin, Paris.

This drawing as well as the following (plates 33-43) is part of a great number of preparatory studies for the large composition of *Bathers* (now in the collection of Carroll S. Tyson, Philadelphia). The painting, the composition of which is based on a relief by Girardon in Versailles, represents the furthest reach of Renoir's effort to escape impressionism and to reestablish a link with the eighteenth century. The artist began to plan the canvas after his return from Italy, in 1882, and labored on it for three years. It was first exhibited in 1887. The preparatory drawings reveal him on the search for a perfect solution of linear harmony and simplification. The present study of a nude and of the folds of a drapery rates among the drawings in which Renoir came closest to Ingres.

33

STUDY FOR "THE BATHERS," 1883
PENCIL, 8⅞ x 11⅞"

Another preparatory drawing for the same figure of a reclining bather.

34

STUDY FOR "THE BATHERS," 1883
PENCIL, 10¼ x 11½"

A detail study for one of the figures of the original composition (see plate 35) The attitude of this bather was later completely changed (see plates 41, 43).

35

STUDY FOR "THE BATHERS," 1883
PASTEL

An aspect of the entire composition which was subsequently simplified and reduced to the large foreground figures (see plates 39-40) and to two small figures in the right background. A painting, done around 1897, which corresponds more closely to this composition than the canvas exhibited in 1887, is in the Barnes Foundation, Merion, Pa.

36

STUDY FOR "THE BATHERS," 1884-85

In this and the following sketch (plate 37) the com
position emerges as centered around three figures.

37

STUDY FOR "THE BATHERS," 1884-85

CRAYON, 8⅝ x 13¾"

38

STUDY FOR "THE BATHERS," 1884-85

Formerly collection A. Vollard, Paris.
A detail study for one of the three main figures (see
also plates 32, 33) in the pose finally adopted.

39

STUDY FOR "THE BATHERS," 1884-85

PENCIL, 9⅜ x 13⅞"

Wadsworth Atheneum, Hartford, Conn.

In this drawing the composition as finally adopted
begins to take shape.

40

STUDY FOR "THE BATHERS," 1884-85

PENCIL, 41 x 64"

Collection J. Laroche, Paris (given to the Louvre).

This large drawing comes closest to the final composition, even in size (the painting is 45¼ x 67"), except for the pose of the central figure, which was to
be nearer that adopted in the drawing above (plate
39).

41

STUDY FOR "THE BATHERS," 1884-85

PENCIL HEIGHTENED WITH WHITE, 38¾ x 25¼"

Collection Mr. and Mrs. Walter S. Brewster,
Chicago.

Study for the right foreground figure, in the scale of
the painting.

42

STUDY FOR "THE BATHERS," 1884-85

Fogg Museum of Art, Cambridge, Mass.
(Maurice Wertheim Collection).

43

STUDY FOR "THE BATHERS," 1884-85

SANGUINE AND BLACK CHALK, HEIGHTENED WITH
WHITE, 34½ x 20½"

Study for the entire right part of the canvas, including the two small bathers in the background.

44

STUDY FOR THE PORTRAIT OF
JULIE MANET, 1887

CRAYON, 24 x 18¼"

Study for a painting dated 1887, representing the
daughter of Berthe Morisot at the age of eight, in
the collection of Mme Ernest Rouart, née Julie
Manet, Paris.

45

YOUNG GIRL WITH A ROSE, 1886

PASTEL, 23½ x 17¼"

There exists a somewhat smaller painting of the bust
of the same girl (18⅞ x 14⅝), belonging to Wildenstein and Co., Inc., New York.

46

LAUNDRESS AND CHILD, c. 1886

PASTEL, 31¾ x 25½"

Private collection, Cleveland.

There exists an unfinished painting of the same subject in the Barnes Foundation, Merion, Pa.

47

MOTHER AND CHILD, c. 1890

SANGUINE HEIGHTENED WITH WHITE, 18¾ x 13"

Fogg Museum of Art, Cambridge, Mass. (Winthrop
Bequest).
The same group appears in a painting, *The Apple
Vender,* in the Barnes Foundation, Merion, Pa.

48

BATHER, 1882-90

PASTEL, 23¾ x 17¾"

49

STUDY SHEET, c. 1885

WATERCOLOR, INK AND PASTEL, 11¾ x 18⅛"

Detroit Institute of Arts.

50

STUDIES OF TREES, c. 1885

PEN AND INK WITH WATERCOLOR, 18¼ x 11¾"

Collection Philip Hofer, Cambridge, Mass.

51

TWO WOMEN WITH A CHILD IN A BOAT, 1883-85

PENCIL AND WATERCOLOR, 9¼ x 7¼"

Collection Philip Hofer, Cambridge, Mass.

52

LA ROCHE-GUYON, 1885-86

53

L'ETANG DE BERRE NEAR MARTIGUES, 1888

PENCIL AND WATERCOLOR, 6½ x 8¾"

54

GIRL WITH A SICKLE, c. 1890

55

BATHER RUBBING HER FOOT, 1885-90

SANGUINE HEIGHTENED WITH WHITE, 14⅜ x 11"

Collection César de Hauke.

56

SEATED BATHER SEEN FROM THE BACK, 1885-90

SANGUINE HEIGHTENED WITH WHITE, 14⅜ x 11"

Collection César de Hauke.

57

WOMAN WITH A BUCKET, c. 1890

CRAYON, 14⅛ x 9⅝"

58

ORANGE VENDER, 1885-90

SANGUINE, 17¾ x 11¾"

A painting of the same subject, painted around 1889, is in the Barnes Foundation, Merion, Pa. The same model, seated, is represented in plate 25.

59

BATHER STANDING, SEEN FROM THE BACK, c. 1890

CRAYON, 12 x 7½"

Collection Mr. and Mrs. H. Lawrence Herring, New York.

Renoir has made a whole series of drawings of this subject, several of which are reproduced in Vollard's book: *La vie et l'oeuvre de Pierre-Auguste Renoir*, Paris, 1919.

60

BATHER STANDING, SEEN FROM THE BACK, c. 1890

Albertina, Vienna.

61

LAUNDRESSES, 1890-95

CRAYON, 16½ x 10⅞"

62

LAUNDRESS AND STUDIES OF CHILDREN, 1890-95

SANGUINE, 14½ x 11"

Collection Paul Rosenberg.

63

LAUNDRESSES, 1887

CRAYON, 11¾ x 8¼"

64

LAUNDRESSES BY THE RIVER, c. 1890

WATERCOLOR, 8⅛ x 6¾"

Cone Collection, Baltimore.

Renoir has repeatedly painted laundresses in attitudes similar to those retained in these four studies (plates 61-64). A canvas corresponding to the composition of this watercolor is in the Cone Collection, Baltimore.

65

MESDEMOISELLES LEROLLE, 1890

CRAYON, 18½ x 24½"

Jacques Seligmann and Co., New York.

Study for a painting representing the two sisters at the piano, in the Durand-Ruel collection. There exist several other preparatory studies for this painting, which is sometimes dated 1898.

66

AT THE PIANO, c. 1890

Galerie Durand-Ruel, Paris.

67

GABRIELLE WITH JEAN RENOIR, c. 1895

PASTEL, 23⅜ x 18"

Gabrielle, the painter's housemaid and favorite model, holds Renoir's second son in her arms. Both appear again, together with Mme Renoir, her oldest son Pierre, and the little daughter of a neighbor, in the large family group painted in 1896, now in the Barnes Foundation, Merion, Pa.

68

THE FLOWERED HAT, c. 1893

PASTEL, 25 x 20"

The models were Berthe Morisot's daughter, Julie Manet, and her young cousin, Paulette Gobillard. This composition seems to have greatly preoccupied the artist, for he made other pastels of the same subject, as well as three etchings and two lithographs (see L. Delteil, op. cit., Nos. 6, 7, 8, 29 and 30).

69

BATHER, 1912

SANGUINE, 23½ x 16⅛"

70

DANCER WITH TAMBOURIN, c. 1912

CRAYON, 46½ x 30"

Collection Louis E. Stern, New York.

A painting of a *Nude with Castanets,* done around 1916 and vaguely related to this drawing, is in the Barnes Foundation, Merion, Pa. This drawing has sometimes been dated 1918.

71

THE JUDGMENT OF PARIS, c. 1908

SANGUINE HEIGHTENED WITH WHITE, 18⅝ x 24⅛"

Phillips Memorial Gallery, Washington, D. C.

There exists a painting of the same subject, dated 1908, for which Gabrielle posed, both as the Paris figure and as the Goddess, at right. Renoir repeated the same composition in several later paintings and in a high-relief which the sculptor Guino executed under his orders. This sanguine is a perfect example of the pictorial effects which Renoir obtained in his late drawings.

72

CHILDREN PLAYING ON THE BEACH, c. 1893

PASTEL

73

PIERRE RENOIR, c. 1896

CRAYON, 11¾ x 10¼"

In the family group of 1896, in the Barnes Foundation, Pierre is also seen in profile with a sailor's cap.

74

PIERRE RENOIR, c. 1896

CRAYON, 15¾ x 12¼"

75

COCO PAINTING, c. 1906

SANGUINE HEIGHTENED WITH WHITE, 23⅝ x 15¾"

76

PORTRAIT OF MLLE S., 1913

CRAYON, 15⅜ x 11¾"

77

GABRIELLE AND COCO, c. 1901

78

CHILD DOING NEEDLE-WORK,
1895-1900

79

PORTRAIT OF A LADY, c. 1905

BLACK CHALK, 23¾ x 17¾"

The portrait is probably of Missia, Renoir's favorite model during his last years.

80

PORTRAIT OF LOUIS VALTAT, 1904

CRAYON, 11⅜ x 9⅝"

Renoir has also done a lithographic portrait of Valtat (see L. Delteil, *op. cit.,* No. 38), which, though closely related to the drawing, lacks its lively directness.

81

BABY SUCKING, 1913

SANGUINE WITH BLACK AND WHITE CHALK, 23¾ x 19½"

Collection Harry A. Woodruff, New York.

82

BABY STANDING, 1913

PASTEL, 24½ x 18½"

Albright Art Gallery, Buffalo, N. Y.

83

BATHER CROUCHING, 1912

CRAYON, 23¼ x 17¾"

84

BATHER DRYING HERSELF, 1912

CRAYON, 24⅜ x 18¾

A painting of a similar subject figured under No. 88 in the Gangnat sale.

85

RHONE AND SAONE, c. 1910

SANGUINE HEIGHTENED WITH WHITE, 24 x 18¾"

These allegorical figures of the two French rivers appear also in a canvas planned as mural decoration. Renoir did two etchings of the same subject, listed under the title *Le Fleuve Scamandre* in L. Delteil, *op. cit.,* Nos. 24, 25.

86

CHLOE, 1912

SANGUINE WITH BLACK CHALK, 24¾ x 18⅛"

87

PORTRAIT OF A YOUNG GIRL,
c. 1906

SANGUINE HEIGHTENED WITH WHITE, 23¼ x 18⅛"
Musée du Louvre, Paris.

88

LAUNDRESSES, 1913

PASTEL, 23¼ x 17¾"

89

SELF PORTRAIT, 1915

CRAYON

Formerly collection A. Vollard, Paris.

The drawing is dedicated: *A Vollard, mon raseur sympathique.*

SOURCES OF ILLUSTRATIONS

Durand-Ruel Galleries, Paris-New York: 1, 5, 6, 7, 8, 15, 28, 30, 31, 32, 33, 35, 37, 43, 44, 45, 46, 48, 53, 57, 58, 59, 61, 62, 63, 67, 68, 69, 73, 74, 76, 79, 80, 83, 85, 86, 88

John D. Schiff, New York: 13, 70, 81

Jacques Seligmann and Co., New York: 4, 20, 64

Justin K. Thannhauser, New York: 26

Valentine Gallery, New York: 66, 71, 75, 77, 78, 84

Vizzavona, Paris: 34, 40, 42, 54, 72

André Weil, Paris-New York: 22, 23

Photographs supplied by owners: 9, 12, 14, 19, 25, 27, 29, 39, 41, 47, 49, 50, 51, 55, 56, 60, 65, 82, 87

The following plates were made after reproductions in A. Vollard: *La vie et l'oeuvre de Pierre-Auguste Renoir,* Paris, 1919: 16, 36, 38, 52, 89

The following plates were made after illustrations in *La Vie Moderne:* 10, 11, 17, 18, 24

PLATES

ARGENTEUIL

c. 1888

6 HEAD OF A YOUNG GIRL

5 HEAD OF A YOUNG GIRL

1875-79   8 HEAD OF A YOUNG GIRL

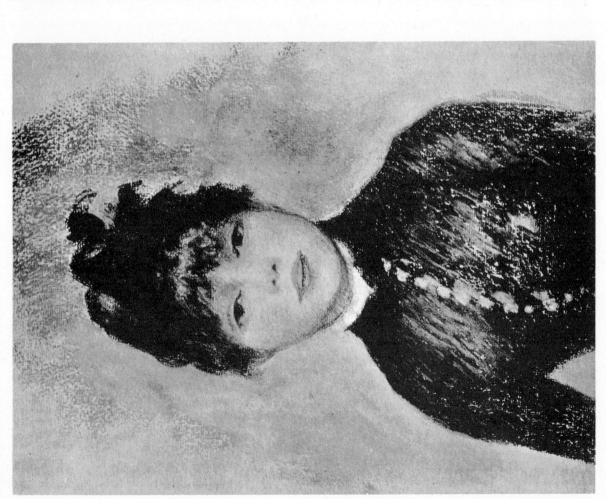

7 HEAD OF A YOUNG GIRL   1875-79

10 ROSITA MAURI IN "LA FARANDOLE"

9 THE DANCER ROSITA MAURI

12 PORTRAIT OF PAUL CEZANNE   1880

11 PORTRAIT OF RICHARD WAGNER   1882-83

16 LA DANSE A LA CAMPAGNE

15 LA DANSE A LA CAMPAGNE

17 LA DANSE A LA CAMPAGNE   1883

18 LA DANSE A LA CAMPAGNE   1883

19 COUPLE IN THE STREET

1883

20 COUPLE ON A HILLSIDE

1883

22 THE BEACH OF GUERNSEY   1883

23 THE BEACH OF GUERNSEY   1883

24 EDMOND RENOIR IN MENTON

1883

25 ORANGE VENDER

26 WOMAN IN A ROCKING CHAIR

27 COPY AFTER MANET'S "FIFRE"   1883

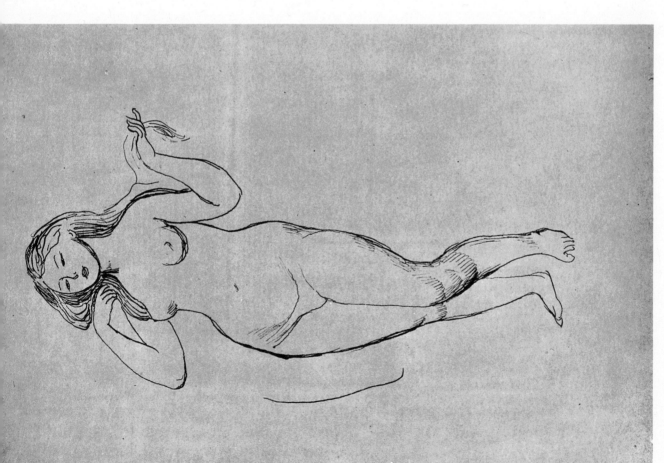

32 STUDY FOR "THE BATHERS"

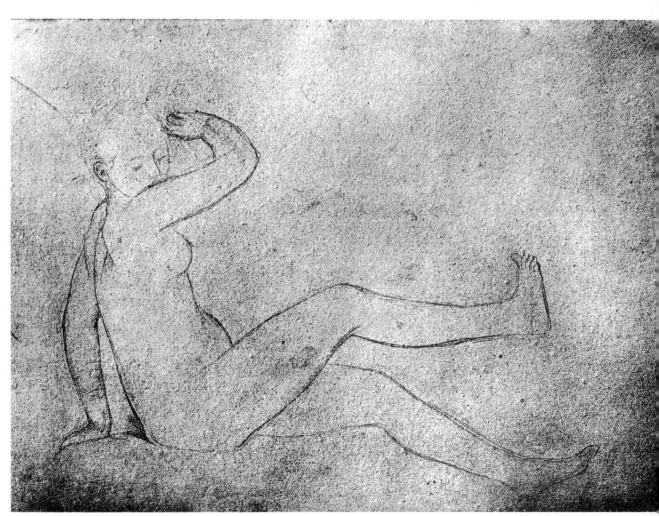

33 STUDY FOR "THE BATHERS"

34 STUDY FOR "THE BATHERS" 1883

STUDY FOR "THE BATHERS" 1883

36 STUDY FOR "THE BATHERS"   1884-85

37 STUDY FOR "THE BATHERS"   1884-

38 STUDY FOR "THE BATHERS" 1884-85

39 STUDY FOR "THE BATHERS" 1884-85

40 STUDY FOR "THE BATHERS" 1884-85

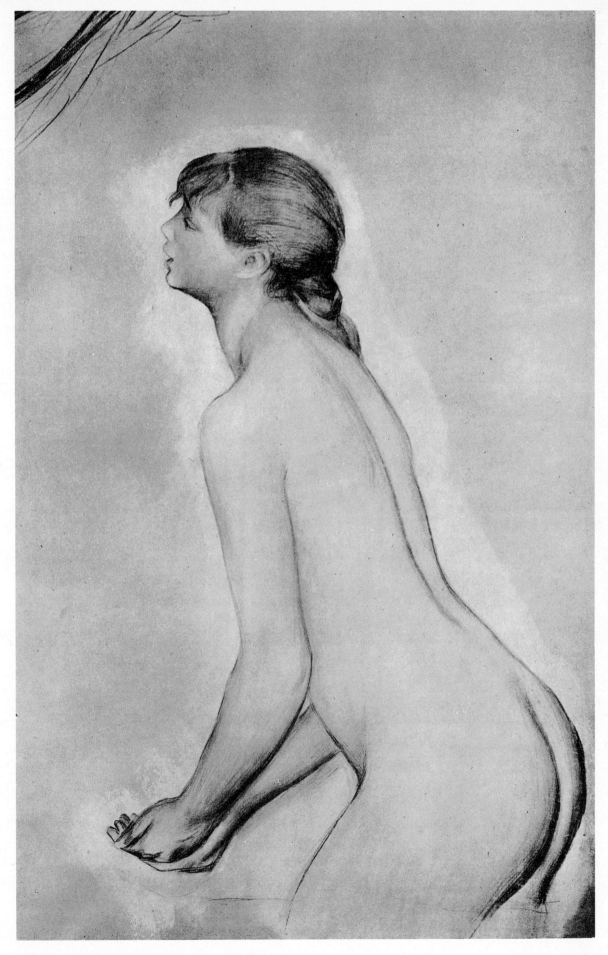

41 STUDY FOR "THE BATHERS"   1884-85

42 STUDY FOR "THE BATHERS"   1884-85

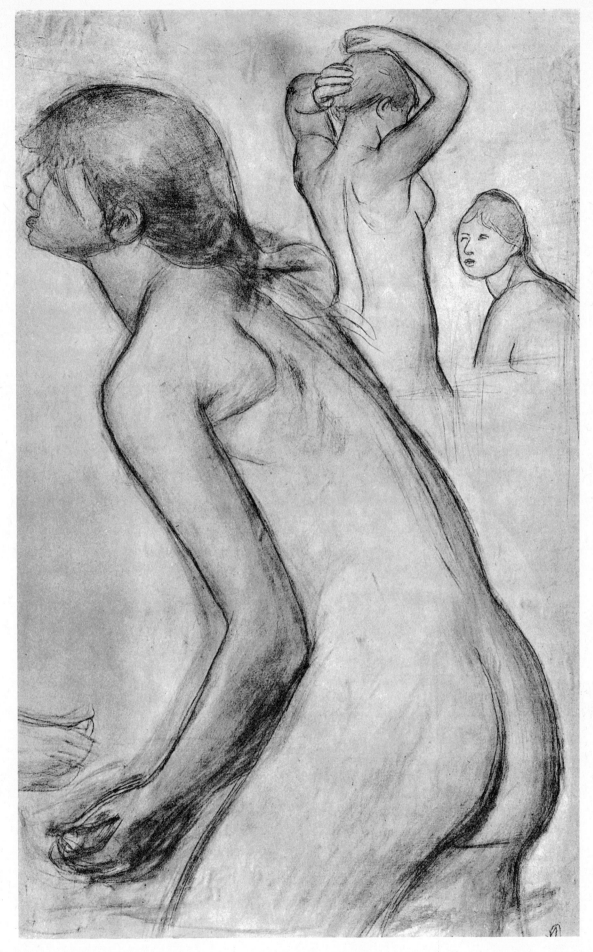

43 STUDY FOR "THE BATHERS"   18478   1884-85

44 STUDY FOR THE PORTRAIT OF JULIE MANET

45 YOUNG GIRL WITH A ROSE

1886

46 LAUNDRESS AND CHILD

c. 1886

47 MOTHER AND CHILD

c. 1890

48 BATHER

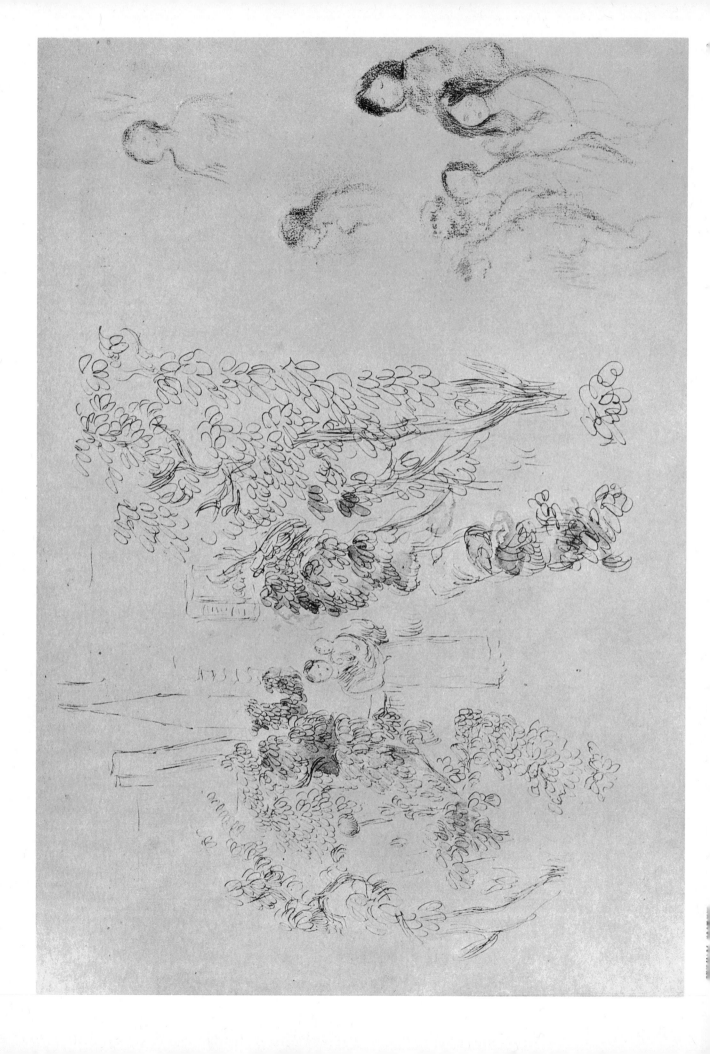

51 TWO WOMEN WITH A CHILD IN A BOAT

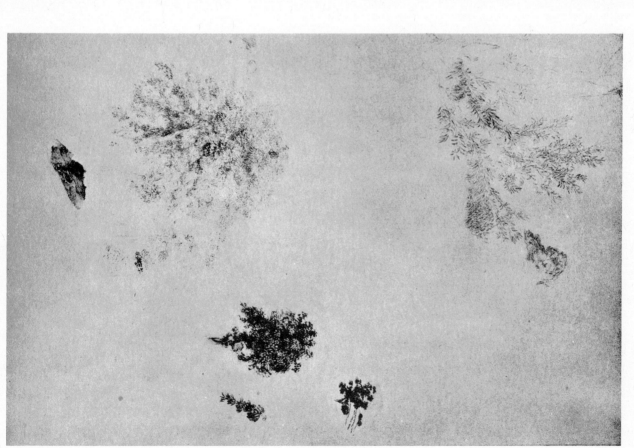

c. 1885

50 STUDIES OF TREES

52 LA ROCHE-GUYON  1885-86

53 L'ETANG DE BERRE NEAR MARTIGUES

54 GIRL WITH SICKLE

c. 1890

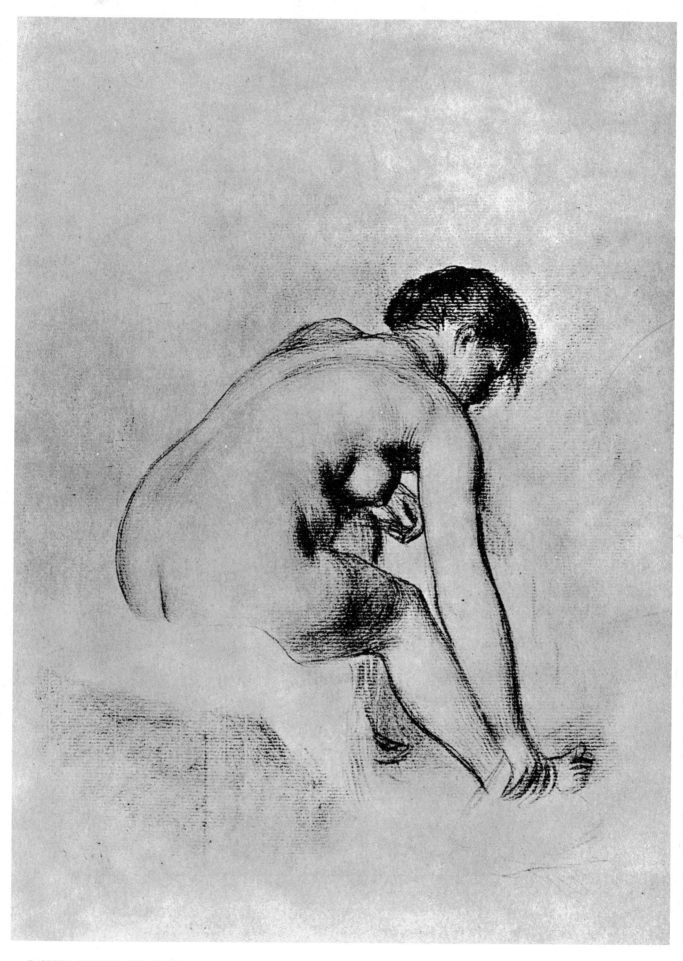

55 BATHER RUBBING HER FOOT   1885-90

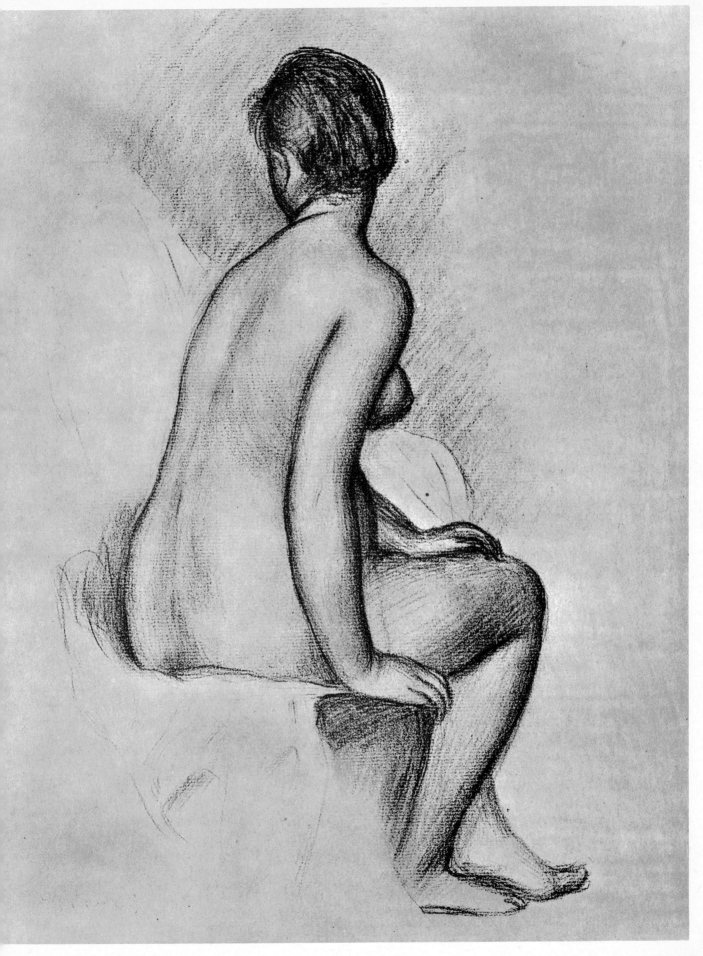

6 SEATED BATHER SEEN FROM THE BACK

1885-90

60 BATHER STANDING, SEEN FROM THE BACK

59 BATHER STANDING, SEEN FROM THE BACK

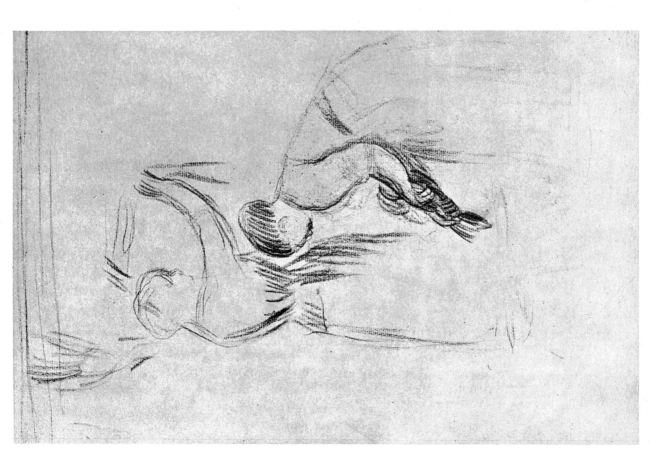

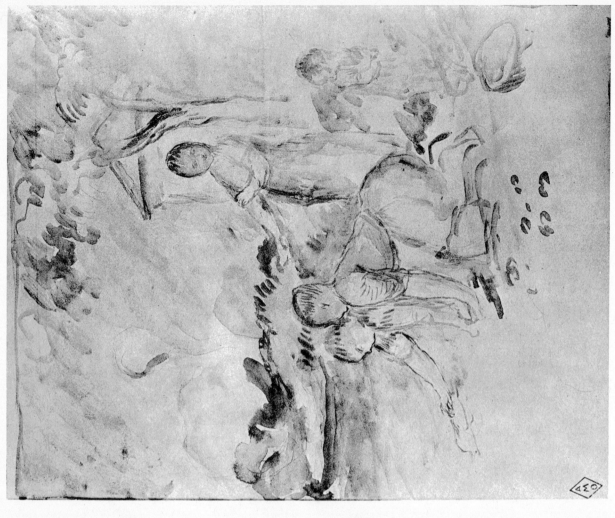

c. 1890   64 LAUNDRESSES BY THE RIVER

1887

63 LAUNDRESSES

65 MESDEMOISELLES LEROLLE

I

66 AT THE PIANO

67 GABRIELLE WITH JEAN RENOIR

c. 1895

68 THE FLOWERED HAT

c. 1893

70 DANCER WITH TAMBOURIN

69 BATHER

71 THE JUDGMENT OF PARIS

CHILDREN PLAYING ON THE BEACH

c. 1893

74 PIERRE RENOIR

73 PIERRE RENOIR   c. 1896

76 PORTRAIT OF MLLE S. 1913

75 COCO PAINTING c. 1906

77 GABRIELLE AND COCO

78 CHILD DOING NEEDLE WORK

1895-1900

79 PORTRAIT OF A LADY

c. 1905

PORTRAIT OF LOUIS VALTAT

81 BABY SUCKING

BABY STANDING   1913

83 BATHER CROUCHING

1912

84 BATHER DRYING HERSELF

1912

85 RHONE AND SOANE

86 CHLOE

87 PORTRAIT OF A YOUNG GIRL

c. 1906